The Power Of Change: Transforming Bad Habits Into Good Ones

Luna Nightingale

Published by Golden Leaf Haven Publishing, 2024.

Table of Contents

Preface

"Welcome to The Power of Change, a transformative journey that will empower you to break free from the limitations of your current habits and unlock a brighter, more fulfilling future. As humans, we are creatures of habit, and our daily routines and behaviors have a profound impact on our overall well-being and quality of life. Yet, so often we find ourselves stuck in patterns of behavior that no longer serve us, holding us back from reaching our full potential.

But what if we told you that change is not only possible, but within your reach? That with the right mindset, tools, and strategies, you can transform your habits and transform your life? In the following pages, we will explore the science and art of habit formation, and provide a comprehensive, step-by-step guide on how to:

- Identify and understand the underlying drivers of your behaviors
- Build a supportive environment that fosters positive change
- Create a personalized plan for transformation
- Overcome obstacles and stay motivated on your journey
- Sustain and reinforce new habits for lasting change

This book is not just about changing your habits, but about changing your life. It's about recognizing that you have the power to choose, to grow, and to become the best version of yourself. It's about unlocking your full potential and living a life that truly reflects your values, aspirations, and dreams.

Through real-life examples, scientific research, and practical exercises, we will show you how to harness the power of change and create a life of purpose, joy, and fulfillment. So, if you're ready to break free from the limitations of your current habits and unlock a brighter future, then join us on this transformative journey. The power of change is within you, and we're here to show you how to tap into it."

The Pitfalls of Overthinking: How Excessive Rumination Can Hold You Back

Overthinking, a common phenomenon in today's fast-paced world, can be a major obstacle to success, happiness, and mental well-being. While thinking and reflection are essential tools for growth and problem-solving, excessive rumination can lead to a cycle of negative thoughts, anxiety, and indecision.

What is Overthinking?

Overthinking, also known as rumination, is the tendency to repetitively think about, analyze, and evaluate thoughts, situations, and emotions. It involves excessive mental chatter, rehashing past events, and worrying about future outcomes. Overthinkers often get caught up in a cycle of "what ifs," "maybes," and "should haves," leading to mental exhaustion and decreased productivity.

Causes of Overthinking

Several factors contribute to overthinking, including:

1. Fear of uncertainty: Fear of the unknown can lead to excessive thinking, as individuals try to control or predict outcomes.
2. Perfectionism: High expectations and self-criticism can fuel overthinking, as individuals strive for flawlessness.
3. Anxiety and stress: High levels of anxiety and stress can trigger rumination, as individuals attempt to cope with their emotions.

4. Trauma: Past traumatic experiences can lead to overthinking, as individuals replay and analyze events.

5. Social media: Social media can foster overthinking, as individuals compare themselves to others and worry about their online presence.

Consequences of Overthinking

Overthinking can have severe consequences, including:

1. Anxiety and depression: Excessive rumination can lead to increased anxiety and depression.

2. Decreased productivity: Overthinking can hinder decision-making and productivity.

3. Strained relationships: Overthinking can lead to misunderstandings, miscommunications, and relationship strain.

4. Physical health problems: Chronic overthinking can contribute to physical health issues, such as headaches, digestive problems, and sleep disturbances.

5. Missed opportunities: Overthinking can cause individuals to miss out on opportunities, as they become mired in indecision.

Strategies for Overcoming Overthinking

Fortunately, there are several strategies to help overcome overthinking:

1. Mindfulness: Practice mindfulness techniques, such as meditation and deep breathing, to calm the mind.

2. Physical activity: Engage in regular exercise to reduce stress and anxiety.

3. Journaling: Write down thoughts and emotions to process and release them.

4. Seek social support: Talk to friends, family, or a therapist about concerns and worries.
5. Practice self-compassion: Treat yourself with kindness, understanding, and patience.
6. Set boundaries: Establish limits on thinking time and engage in activities that bring joy.
7. Challenge negative thoughts: Question and reframe negative, distorted, or unhelpful thinking patterns.

Overthinking can be a major obstacle to success, happiness, and mental well-being. By understanding the causes, consequences, and strategies for overcoming overthinking, individuals can break free from the cycle of excessive rumination and cultivate a more balanced, productive, and fulfilling life. Remember, thinking is essential, but overthinking can be detrimental. Learn to strike a healthy balance and live a more mindful, compassionate, and joyful life.

The Perils of Procrastination: Understanding the Habit and Breaking Free

Procrastination, a habit that affects millions, can lead to missed deadlines, lost opportunities, and decreased productivity.

What is Procrastination?

Procrastination is the intentional delay or postponement of tasks or decisions, often leading to feelings of guilt, stress, and lost productivity. It involves prioritizing non-essential activities over important tasks, causing individuals to fall behind and struggle to catch up.

Causes of Procrastination

Several factors contribute to procrastination, including:

1. Fear of failure: Fear of not meeting expectations or fear of failure can lead to procrastination.
2. Perfectionism: High expectations and self-criticism can cause individuals to delay starting tasks.
3. Lack of motivation: Insufficient motivation or unclear goals can lead to procrastination.
4. Distractions: Modern technology and social media can provide endless distractions, making it difficult to focus.
5. Time management: Poor time management skills can lead to procrastination and decreased productivity.

Consequences of Procrastination

Procrastination can have severe consequences, including:

1. Missed deadlines: Delayed tasks can lead to missed deadlines and lost opportunities.
2. Decreased productivity: Procrastination can significantly decrease productivity and efficiency.
3. Increased stress: Last-minute rushes and missed deadlines can lead to increased stress levels.
4. Strained relationships: Procrastination can lead to strained relationships with colleagues, friends, and family.
5. Lost opportunities: Procrastination can cause individuals to miss out on opportunities and experiences.

Strategies for Overcoming Procrastination

Fortunately, there are several strategies to help overcome procrastination:

1. Break tasks into smaller steps: Divide large tasks into smaller, manageable steps.
2. Set clear goals and deadlines: Establish clear goals and deadlines to increase motivation.
3. Use the Pomodoro Technique: Work in focused 25-minute increments, followed by a 5-minute break.
4. Remove distractions: Eliminate or limit distractions, such as turning off notifications.
5. Create a schedule: Plan out your day, week, or month to increase productivity.

6. Seek accountability: Share goals and progress with a friend or mentor to increase motivation.

7. Practice self-compassion: Treat yourself with kindness and understanding when making mistakes.

8. Reward progress: Celebrate small victories to increase motivation.

Procrastination is a habit that can be overcome with understanding, strategies, and practice. By recognizing the causes and consequences of procrastination, individuals can take steps to break free from this cycle and achieve their goals. Remember, overcoming procrastination is a process that takes time, effort, and patience. Start today, and take the first step towards a more productive, successful, and fulfilling life.

The Dangers of Smoking: A Deadly Habit That Affects Us All

Smoking, a habit that has been prevalent for centuries, poses a significant threat to human health, causing millions of deaths worldwide each year.

History of Smoking

Smoking has its roots in ancient civilizations, where tobacco was first consumed over 2,000 years ago. However, it wasn't until the 20th century that smoking became a widespread habit, with the introduction of mass-produced cigarettes.

Health Risks of Smoking

Smoking is a leading cause of preventable deaths worldwide, accounting for over seven million fatalities annually. The health risks associated with smoking are numerous and well-documented, including:

1. Lung Cancer: Smoking is the leading cause of lung cancer, responsible for approximately 80% of all lung cancer deaths.
2. Heart Disease: Smoking damages cardiovascular health, increasing the risk of heart attacks, strokes, and other cardiovascular diseases.
3. Chronic Obstructive Pulmonary Disease (COPD): Smoking can cause COPD, a progressive lung disease that makes breathing difficult.
4. Other Cancers: Smoking is linked to an increased risk of several other cancers, including throat, mouth, and bladder cancer.

Secondhand Smoke

Secondhand smoke, also known as passive smoking, poses a significant risk to non-smokers. Exposure to secondhand smoke can lead to:

1. Respiratory Problems: Secondhand smoke can cause respiratory issues, such as asthma and bronchitis.
2. Increased Cancer Risk: Secondhand smoke exposure increases the risk of developing lung cancer and other cancers.
3. Cardiovascular Disease: Secondhand smoke exposure can lead to cardiovascular disease and heart attacks.

Quitting Smoking

Quitting smoking is a challenging task, but it's not impossible. Strategies for quitting include:

1. Nicotine Replacement Therapy (NRT): NRT can help manage withdrawal symptoms and cravings.
2. Counseling: One-on-one counseling or support groups can provide motivation and guidance.
3. Prescription Medications: Prescription medications, such as bupropion and varenicline, can help manage cravings and withdrawal symptoms.
4. Healthy Habits: Engaging in healthy habits, such as exercise and meditation, can help manage stress and cravings.

Smoking is a deadly habit that affects us all, whether directly or indirectly. Understanding the risks and consequences of smoking is crucial in making informed decisions about our health. Quitting smoking is a journey that requires patience, persistence, and support. If you're a smoker, consider quitting today and take the first step towards a healthier, smoke-free life.

The Dangers of Overeating: A Growing Health Concern

Overeating, a habit that affects millions worldwide, poses a significant threat to our health and wellbeing.

Causes of Overeating

Overeating can stem from various factors, including:

1. Emotional Eating: Using food as a coping mechanism for emotions like stress, anxiety, or sadness.
2. Lack of Mindful Eating: Failing to pay attention to hunger and fullness cues, leading to excessive food consumption.
3. Unhealthy Relationships with Food: Using food as a reward or punishment, or having a restrictive diet that leads to bingeing.
4. Genetic Predisposition: Genetic factors can influence appetite regulation and metabolism.
5. Societal Pressures: Exposure to unhealthy food marketing and social norms that promote overconsumption.

Consequences of Overeating

Overeating can lead to:

1. Weight Gain and Obesity: Consuming more calories than needed, resulting in weight gain and obesity.

2. Increased Risk of Chronic Diseases: Higher risk of developing conditions like diabetes, heart disease, and certain cancers.

3. Nutrient Imbalance: Overeating can lead to an imbalance of essential nutrients, causing deficiencies and health problems.

4. Mental Health Concerns: Overeating can contribute to depression, anxiety, and low self-esteem.

5. Digestive Issues: Overeating can cause discomfort, bloating, and digestive problems.

Strategies for Overcoming Overeating

Breaking the cycle of overeating requires a comprehensive approach:

1. Mindful Eating: Pay attention to hunger and fullness cues, savor food, and eat slowly.

2. Healthy Portion Control: Learn to recognize and control serving sizes.

3. Balanced Nutrition: Focus on whole, nutrient-dense foods, and limit processed and high-calorie foods.

4. Emotional Regulation: Develop healthy coping mechanisms for emotions, such as exercise, meditation, or journaling.

5. Seek Support: Consult a registered dietitian, therapist, or support group for guidance and accountability.

Overeating is a complex issue that affects individuals and society as a whole. By understanding the causes, consequences, and strategies for overcoming overeating, we can take the first step towards a healthier relationship with food and our bodies. Remember, breaking the cycle of overeating takes time, patience, and self-compassion. Start your journey today and cultivate a balanced, nourishing relationship with food.

The Dark Side of Screen Time: Understanding the Risks of Excessive Screen Use

In today's digital age, screens are an integral part of our daily lives. From smartphones and tablets to computers and televisions, we are constantly surrounded by screens. While screens have revolutionized the way we communicate, work, and entertain ourselves, excessive screen time can have serious consequences for our physical and mental health.

The Risks of Excessive Screen Time

Excessive screen time has been linked to a range of health problems, including:

1. Sleep Disturbances: Exposure to screens before bed can disrupt sleep patterns and reduce sleep quality.
2. Eye Strain and Vision Problems: Prolonged screen time can cause eye strain, dry eyes, and increase the risk of myopia and hyperopia.
3. Sedentary Behavior: Excessive screen time can lead to a sedentary lifestyle, contributing to obesity, diabetes, and cardiovascular disease.
4. Mental Health Concerns: Excessive screen time has been linked to increased symptoms of depression, anxiety, and loneliness.
5. Social Isolation: Excessive screen time can lead to social isolation, decreased face-to-face interaction, and reduced empathy.
6. Addiction: Excessive screen time can lead to screen addiction, a condition characterized by compulsive screen use despite negative consequences.

The Impact on Children and Teenagers

Excessive screen time can have particularly devastating effects on children and teenagers, including:

1. Delayed Cognitive Development: Excessive screen time can delay cognitive development, including attention, memory, and problem-solving skills.
2. Increased Risk of Obesity: Excessive screen time can contribute to obesity and related health problems.
3. Mental Health Concerns: Excessive screen time can increase symptoms of depression, anxiety, and loneliness in children and teenagers.
4. Social Skills Deficits: Excessive screen time can lead to social skills deficits, including decreased empathy and face-to-face interaction skills.

Strategies for Reducing Screen Time

Reducing screen time requires a comprehensive approach:

1. Set Screen-Free Zones: Designate screen-free zones, such as the bedroom or dining table.
2. Establish Screen-Free Times: Establish screen-free times, such as during meals or before bed.
3. Use Screen Time Tracking Tools: Use tools to track screen time and set limits.
4. Encourage Physical Activity: Encourage physical activity and outdoor play.
5. Promote Alternative Activities: Promote alternative activities, such as reading, drawing, or hobbies.

Excessive screen time is a serious health concern that demands attention and action. By understanding the risks and implementing strategies to reduce screen time, we can protect our physical and mental health. Remember, a balanced and healthy lifestyle is just a screen away.

The Poison of Gossip: How Rumors and Slander Can Destroy Lives

Gossiping, a ubiquitous and insidious behavior, can have far-reaching and devastating consequences.

The Definition and Prevalence of Gossip

Gossiping refers to the act of sharing personal or sensational information about others, often without their consent or knowledge. Gossip can take many forms, from casual conversations to social media posts. Unfortunately, gossiping is a widespread behavior, with studies suggesting that up to 80% of conversations involve gossip.

The Consequences of Gossiping

Gossiping can have severe consequences, including:

1. Damaged Relationships: Gossip can erode trust, ruin friendships, and destroy reputations.
2. Emotional Distress: Gossip can cause significant emotional pain, anxiety, and depression.
3. Social Exclusion: Gossip can lead to social exclusion, ostracism, and feelings of isolation.
4. Loss of Productivity: Gossip can distract from important tasks, reducing productivity and efficiency.
5. Community Division: Gossip can create divisions within communities, fostering a culture of suspicion and mistrust.

Why Do People Gossip?

Understanding the motivations behind gossiping can help us address this behavior:

1. Social Bonding: Gossip can create a sense of belonging and social connection.
2. Power Dynamics: Gossip can be used to assert power or control over others.
3. Boredom and Entertainment: Gossip can provide a thrilling distraction from mundane routines.
4. Lack of Empathy: Gossip can stem from a lack of understanding or empathy for others.

Strategies for Combating Gossip

Breaking the cycle of gossip requires a collective effort:

1. Practice Empathy and Understanding: Put yourself in others' shoes and try to see things from their perspective.
2. Set Boundaries: Establish clear boundaries around what is and isn't acceptable conversation.
3. Encourage Positive Communication: Foster a culture of open, honest, and respectful communication.
4. Address Gossip Directly: Confront gossipers and encourage them to refrain from spreading rumors.
5. Model Good Behavior: Demonstrate respectful and empathetic behavior, inspiring others to do the same.

Gossiping is a toxic behavior that can have far-reaching and devastating consequences. By understanding the motivations behind gossiping and implementing strategies to combat it, we can create a more compassionate and respectful environment. Remember, words have power – let's use them to uplift and support each other, rather than tear each other down.

The Deceptive Nature of Lying: Understanding the Consequences and Impact

Lying, a ubiquitous and complex behavior, can have far-reaching and devastating consequences.

Defining Lying

Lying refers to the intentional act of communicating false information with the intention of deceiving or misleading others. Lying can take many forms, from white lies and exaggerations to outright fabrications and deception.

Types of Lies

Lies can be categorized into several types, including:

1. White Lies: Harmless, trivial lies told to avoid hurting someone's feelings or maintain social harmony.
2. Exaggerations: Stretching the truth to emphasize a point or achieve a desired effect.
3. Omissions: Withholding information to create a false impression or conceal the truth.
4. Fabrications: Completely made-up lies with no basis in reality.
5. Deception: Intentionally misleading or deceiving others through words or actions.

Motivations for Lying

Understanding why people lie can help us address this behavior:

1. Fear and Anxiety: Lying to avoid punishment, rejection, or conflict.
2. Self-Protection: Lying to protect oneself from harm, criticism, or vulnerability.
3. Personal Gain: Lying to achieve personal benefits, such as financial gain or social status.
4. Social Pressure: Lying to conform to social norms or avoid social exclusion.
5. Habitual Behavior: Lying as a deeply ingrained habit or automatic response.

Consequences of Lying

Lying can have severe consequences, including:
1. Eroding Trust: Lying can damage relationships, erode trust, and destroy credibility.
2. Emotional Distress: Lying can cause significant emotional pain, anxiety, and stress.
3. Social Consequences: Lying can lead to social exclusion, ostracism, and reputational damage.
4. Legal Consequences: Lying can result in legal repercussions, fines, and imprisonment.
5. Internal Conflict: Lying can lead to internal conflict, guilt, and self-doubt.

Detecting Lies

Detecting lies requires attention to verbal and nonverbal cues:

1. Body Language: Inconsistencies in body language, such as avoiding eye contact or fidgeting.

2. Verbal Cues: Inconsistencies in speech, such as hesitations, contradictions, or evasions.

3. Emotional Incongruence: Inconsistencies between emotional expressions and verbal statements.

4. Inconsistencies: Inconsistencies in stories, alibis, or explanations.

Preventing Lies

Preventing lies requires a culture of honesty, transparency, and accountability:

1. Encourage Open Communication: Foster an environment where open, honest communication is encouraged.

2. Set Clear Expectations: Establish clear expectations and consequences for dishonesty.

3. Model Honest Behavior: Demonstrate honest behavior and integrity in leadership and role models.

4. Address Lies Directly: Confront lies directly and address the underlying motivations and behaviors.

Lying is a complex and multifaceted behavior with far-reaching consequences. By understanding the motivations, consequences, and strategies for detection and prevention, we can create a culture of honesty, transparency, and accountability. Remember, honesty is the foundation of trust, respect, and strong relationships – let's cultivate a culture of truthfulness and integrity.

The Consequences of Wasting Resources: A Growing Concern for Our Planet

Wasting resources, a ubiquitous and reckless behavior, poses a significant threat to our planet's sustainability.

Types of Resource Waste

Resource waste can be categorized into several types, including:

1. Water Waste: Wasting water through leaks, inefficient appliances, and unnecessary usage.
2. Energy Waste: Wasting energy through inefficient lighting, heating, and cooling systems.
3. Food Waste: Wasting food through overproduction, spoilage, and unnecessary disposal.
4. Material Waste: Wasting materials through single-use plastics, paper, and other disposable products.
5. Land Waste: Wasting land through deforestation, urbanization, and inefficient agriculture.

Consequences of Resource Waste

Resource waste has severe consequences, including:

1. Environmental Degradation: Resource waste contributes to pollution, climate change, and ecosystem destruction.

2. Economic Burden: Resource waste results in significant economic losses, wasted investments, and reduced productivity.

3. Social Injustice: Resource waste perpetuates social injustices, as marginalized communities often bear the brunt of environmental degradation.

4. Health Risks: Resource waste poses health risks, as pollution and waste can lead to respiratory problems, cancer, and other diseases.

Strategies for Reduction and Conservation

Reducing and conserving resources requires a multifaceted approach:

1. Increase Efficiency: Implement efficient technologies, practices, and systems to reduce waste.

2. Reduce Consumption: Encourage reduced consumption through education, awareness, and behavioral change.

3. Reuse and Recycle: Promote reuse and recycling of materials to minimize waste.

4. Implement Sustainable Practices: Encourage sustainable agriculture, forestry, and land use practices.

5. Develop Circular Economies: Foster circular economies that prioritize resource reuse, recycling, and minimization of waste.

Individual Actions

Individuals can make a significant impact by:

1. Reducing Water Usage: Fixing leaks, using efficient appliances, and taking shorter showers.

2. Using Energy-Efficient Appliances: Replacing traditional incandescent bulbs with LED bulbs and using energy-efficient appliances.

3. Planning Meals and Reducing Food Waste: Planning meals, using up leftovers, and composting food waste.

4. Avoiding Single-Use Plastics: Refusing single-use plastics, carrying reusable bags, and using refillable containers.

5. Supporting Sustainable Practices: Supporting organizations, policies, and practices that prioritize resource conservation.

Wasting resources is a pressing concern that demands attention and action. By understanding the types of resource waste, its consequences, and strategies for reduction and conservation, we can work towards a more sustainable future. Remember, every small action counts, and collective efforts can lead to significant positive change.

The Myth of Multitasking: How Trying to Do it All Can Actually Reduce Productivity

Multitasking, a term coined in the 1960s, has become a ubiquitous concept in today's fast-paced world. Many of us pride ourselves on our ability to multitask, juggling multiple tasks simultaneously with ease. However, research suggests that multitasking may not be the productivity booster we think it is. In fact, trying to do it all can actually reduce productivity, increase stress, and decrease overall performance.

The Myth of Multitasking

Multitasking is often misunderstood as the ability to perform multiple tasks simultaneously. However, in reality, our brains can only focus on one task at a time. What we're actually doing when we multitask is task-switching, rapidly switching between tasks without fully focusing on any one task.

The Consequences of Multitasking

Multitasking can have severe consequences, including:

1. Reduced Productivity: Multitasking can decrease productivity by up to 40%, as our brains struggle to switch between tasks.
2. Increased Stress: Multitasking can lead to increased stress levels, as we try to juggle multiple tasks and deadlines.
3. Decreased Attention Span: Multitasking can reduce our attention span, making it difficult to focus on one task for an extended period.

4. Increased Errors: Multitasking can lead to increased errors, as our brains struggle to keep track of multiple tasks.

The Benefits of Single-Tasking

Single-tasking, on the other hand, offers numerous benefits, including:

1. Increased Productivity: Focusing on one task at a time can increase productivity by up to 50%.

2. Improved Quality: Single-tasking can lead to improved quality, as our brains can focus on the task at hand.

3. Reduced Stress: Single-tasking can reduce stress levels, as we're only focusing on one task.

4. Improved Attention Span: Single-tasking can improve our attention span, allowing us to focus on one task for an extended period.

Strategies for Single-Tasking

To incorporate single-tasking into your daily routine, try the following strategies:

1. Prioritize Tasks: Prioritize tasks based on importance and deadlines.

2. Focus on One Task: Focus on one task at a time, eliminating distractions.

3. Use Time Blocking: Use time blocking to dedicate specific times to specific tasks.

4. Take Breaks: Take breaks between tasks to recharge and refocus.

Multitasking is a myth that can actually reduce productivity, increase stress, and decrease overall performance. By incorporating single-tasking into our daily routine, we can improve productivity, quality, and attention span, while reducing stress and errors. Remember, focusing on one task at a time is the key to achieving success in today's fast-paced world.

The Dangers of Negative Self-Talk: How Criticizing Yourself Can Hold You Back

Negative self-talk, a pervasive and insidious behavior, can have far-reaching consequences on our mental health, self-esteem, and overall well-being.

What is Negative Self-Talk?

Negative self-talk refers to the critical, demeaning, and discouraging thoughts we direct towards ourselves. These thoughts can be verbal or non-verbal, conscious or unconscious, and can manifest in various ways, such as:

1. Self-Criticism: Criticizing oneself for mistakes, shortcomings, or perceived flaws.
2. Self-Doubt: Questioning one's abilities, judgment, or decision-making.
3. Self-Blame: Attributing failures or setbacks to personal inadequacies.
4. Self-Comparison: Comparing oneself unfavorably to others.

The Consequences of Negative Self-Talk

Negative self-talk can lead to:

1. Low Self-Esteem: Eroding confidence, self-worth, and self-acceptance.
2. Anxiety and Depression: Contributing to the development of anxiety and depression.
3. Self-Sabotage: Undermining goals, aspirations, and progress.

4. Strained Relationships: Damaging relationships through self-doubt, defensiveness, and negativity.

Why Do We Engage in Negative Self-Talk?

Understanding the motivations behind negative self-talk can help us address this behavior:

1. Past Experiences: Negative self-talk can stem from past criticisms, traumas, or negative experiences.
2. Fear of Failure: Fear of failure can lead to self-doubt and negative self-talk.
3. Perfectionism: Unrealistic expectations can foster self-criticism and negative self-talk.
4. Social Comparison: Comparing oneself to others can lead to negative self-talk and self-doubt.

Overcoming Negative Self-Talk

Breaking the cycle of negative self-talk requires:

1. Self-Awareness: Recognizing negative self-talk patterns and their triggers.
2. Self-Compassion: Practicing kindness, understanding, and patience towards oneself.
3. Reframing Negative Thoughts: Challenging and replacing negative thoughts with balanced, realistic ones.
4. Building Self-Esteem: Fostering self-acceptance, self-worth, and confidence through positive experiences and affirmations.

Negative self-talk is a damaging habit that can hold us back from reaching our full potential. By understanding its consequences, motivations, and strategies for overcoming it, we can break free from this cycle of negativity and cultivate a more compassionate, supportive relationship with ourselves. Remember, our thoughts have power – let's use them to uplift and empower ourselves.

The Dangers of Overspending: How Breaking the Cycle Can Lead to Financial Freedom

Overspending, a pervasive and often unconscious behavior, can lead to financial stress, debt, and a reduced quality of life.

Causes of Overspending

Overspending can stem from various factors, including:

1. Emotional Spending: Using shopping as a coping mechanism for emotions like stress, boredom, or anxiety.
2. Social Pressure: Feeling pressure to keep up with others' spending habits or lifestyles.
3. Lack of Budgeting: Failing to track expenses or create a realistic budget.
4. Instant Gratification: Prioritizing short-term wants over long-term financial goals.
5. Marketing Manipulation: Succumbing to persuasive advertising and sales tactics.

Consequences of Overspending

Overspending can lead to:

1. Debt Accumulation: Credit card debt, loans, and other financial obligations.

2. *Financial Stress: Anxiety, worry, and feelings of overwhelm related to financial situation.*

3. *Reduced Savings: Insufficient funds for emergencies, retirement, or long-term goals.*

4. *Opportunity Costs: Missing out on investments, experiences, or personal growth due to excessive spending.*

5. *Damaged Credit Scores: Negative impact on credit scores, limiting future financial options.*

Strategies for Overcoming Overspending

Breaking the cycle of overspending requires:

1. *Self-Awareness: Recognizing spending habits, triggers, and motivations.*

2. *Budgeting and Tracking: Creating a realistic budget and monitoring expenses.*

3. *Prioritization: Focusing on essential expenses and long-term financial goals.*

4. *Delayed Gratification: Practicing patience and waiting for needs to arise before spending.*

5. *Mindful Spending: Making intentional, conscious purchasing decisions.*

6. *Seeking Support: Consulting financial advisors, therapists, or support groups for guidance.*

Additional Tips for Success

1. *Implement a 30-Day Rule: Waiting 30 days before making non-essential purchases.*

2. *Use Cash: Paying with cash to increase awareness of spending.*

3. *Avoid Temptation: Limiting exposure to shopping centers, online retailers, or sales.*

4. Cultivate Gratitude: Focusing on existing possessions and experiences.
5. Celebrate Milestones: Acknowledging progress and achievements along the way.

Overspending is a common obstacle to financial freedom, but it can be overcome. By understanding the causes, consequences, and strategies for breaking the cycle, individuals can develop healthier relationships with money and achieve peace of mind. Remember, financial freedom is within reach – take the first step today.

The Consequences of Not Listening Actively: How Passive Hearing Can Lead to Misunderstandings and Missed Opportunities

Active listening, a crucial skill in personal and professional settings, is often overlooked and underpracticed.

The Consequences of Not Listening Actively

Not listening actively can lead to:

1. Misunderstandings: Misinterpreting information, leading to errors, conflicts, and missed opportunities.
2. Missed Opportunities: Failing to grasp new ideas, perspectives, or insights, hindering personal and professional growth.
3. Strained Relationships: Damaging relationships through lack of understanding, empathy, and engagement.
4. Inefficient Communication: Wasting time and resources due to unclear or misunderstood instructions.
5. Decreased Productivity: Reducing productivity and performance through lack of clear direction and understanding.

Passive Hearing vs. Active Listening

Passive hearing involves:

1. Hearing Words: Only registering the surface-level meaning of words.
2. Not Engaging: Failing to engage with the speaker, ask questions, or clarify doubts.
3. Distracted Listening: Allowing distractions to divert attention away from the speaker.

Active listening involves:

1. Engaging with the Speaker: Maintaining eye contact, nodding, and asking questions.
2. Paraphrasing and Summarizing: Repeating back what was heard to ensure understanding.
3. Asking Clarifying Questions: Seeking additional information to clarify doubts.
4. Providing Feedback: Offering thoughts, opinions, and insights in response.

Strategies for Improving Listening Skills

1. Practice Mindfulness: Being present and focused on the speaker.
2. Set Aside Distractions: Eliminating or minimizing distractions during conversations.
3. Use Verbal and Nonverbal Cues: Encouraging the speaker through nods, eye contact, and verbal affirmations.
4. Take Notes: Recording key points and ideas to reference later.
5. Seek Feedback: Asking speakers if they feel heard and understood.

Not listening actively can have far-reaching consequences, from misunderstandings and missed opportunities to strained relationships and decreased productivity. By understanding the differences between passive hearing and active listening and implementing strategies for improvement, individuals can become better listeners, leading to stronger relationships, improved communication, and increased success. Remember, active listening is a skill that can be developed with practice and patience.

The Weight of Holding Grudges: How Letting Go Can Free Your Mind and Heart

Holding grudges, a common yet toxic behavior, can consume our thoughts, emotions, and relationships.

The Consequences of Holding Grudges

Holding grudges can lead to:

1. Emotional Turmoil: Persistent feelings of anger, resentment, and bitterness.
2. Strained Relationships: Damaged connections with others, causing isolation and loneliness.
3. Mental Health Issues: Increased stress, anxiety, and depression.
4. Physical Health Problems: Weakened immune system, cardiovascular disease, and chronic pain.
5. Missed Opportunities: Holding onto grudges can prevent personal growth, new experiences, and meaningful connections.

Why We Struggle to Let Go

1. Fear of Vulnerability: Letting go of grudges requires vulnerability and openness.
2. Sense of Control: Holding grudges provides a false sense of control and power.

3. *Lack of Empathy:* Struggling to understand the other person's perspective and humanity.
4. *Past Trauma:* Unresolved trauma can make it difficult to release grudges.
5. *Social and Cultural Norms:* Societal expectations and cultural norms can encourage holding grudges.

The Power of Forgiveness

Forgiveness is not:

1. *Forgetting:* Forgiveness doesn't erase the past or excuse hurtful behavior.
2. *Condoning:* Forgiveness doesn't justify or condone wrongdoing.
3. *Reconciling:* Forgiveness doesn't require reconciliation or reunification.

Forgiveness is:

1. *Letting Go:* Releasing the emotional burden of grudges.
2. *Healing:* Allowing yourself to heal and move forward.
3. *Empowering:* Taking control of your emotions and well-being.
4. *Liberating:* Freeing yourself from the weight of resentment and anger.

Strategies for Letting Go

1. *Acknowledge and Accept:* Recognize the hurt and accept your emotions.
2. *Empathize and Understand:* Try to see the other person's perspective and humanity.
3. *Practice Self-Compassion:* Treat yourself with kindness, care, and patience.
4. *Seek Support:* Reach out to trusted friends, family, or professionals for guidance.

5. Cultivate Mindfulness: Focus on the present moment and let go of negative thoughts.

Holding grudges can weigh heavily on our minds and hearts, causing emotional turmoil, strained relationships, and missed opportunities. By understanding the reasons we struggle to let go and embracing the power of forgiveness, we can release the burden of grudges and move towards healing, growth, and liberation. Remember, forgiveness is a journey, and letting go is a process – take the first step today.

The Devastating Consequences of Neglecting Self-Care: Why Prioritizing Your Own Needs is Essential

In today's fast-paced world, it's easy to get caught up in the hustle and bustle of daily life and neglect one of the most important aspects of our overall well-being: self-care. Neglecting self-care can have severe consequences on our physical, emotional, and mental health, relationships, and overall quality of life.

The Consequences of Neglecting Self-Care

Neglecting self-care can lead to:

1. Burnout: Physical, emotional, and mental exhaustion.
2. Chronic Stress: Increased risk of anxiety, depression, and other mental health issues.
3. Weakened Immune System: Increased susceptibility to illnesses and diseases.
4. Strained Relationships: Damaged connections with loved ones due to irritability, mood swings, and lack of emotional availability.
5. Decreased Productivity: Reduced focus, motivation, and performance in work and personal life.
6. Poor Physical Health: Neglect of physical needs leading to weight gain, sleep disturbances, and other health problems.
7. Mental Health Issues: Increased risk of depression, anxiety, and other mental health issues.

Why We Neglect Self-Care

1. Societal Pressures: Expectations to prioritize others' needs over our own.
2. Fear of Selfishness: Believing self-care is selfish or indulgent.
3. Lack of Time: Feeling too busy to prioritize self-care.
4. Unrealistic Expectations: Setting unachievable standards for ourselves.
5. Trauma and Past Experiences: Neglecting self-care due to past traumas or experiences.

Prioritizing Self-Care

1. Schedule Self-Care: Treat self-care as a non-negotiable part of your daily routine.
2. Listen to Your Body: Pay attention to physical and emotional needs.
3. Set Boundaries: Learn to say "no" and prioritize your own needs.
4. Practice Mindfulness: Focus on the present moment and let go of stress.
5. Seek Support: Surround yourself with people who support and encourage self-care.

Neglecting self-care can have severe consequences on our overall well-being, relationships, and quality of life. By understanding the importance of self-care and making it a priority, we can avoid burnout, chronic stress, and other negative consequences. Remember, taking care of yourself is not selfish – it's essential. Start prioritizing your own needs today and experience the transformative power of self-care.

The Chronic Consequences of Consistent Lateness: How Tardiness Affects Your Life and Relationships

Consistent lateness, a habitual behavior for many, can have far-reaching consequences on our personal and professional lives, relationships, and overall well-being.

The Consequences of Consistent Lateness

Consistent lateness can lead to:

1. Damaged Relationships: Strained connections with family, friends, and colleagues due to unreliability and disrespect.
2. Professional Consequences: Missed opportunities, lost productivity, and damaged reputation.
3. Increased Stress: Rushing to meet deadlines, feeling anxious, and experiencing burnout.
4. Poor Time Management: Inefficient use of time, leading to missed appointments and deadlines.
5. Lack of Accountability: Blaming external circumstances rather than taking responsibility for tardiness.
6. Negative Self-Image: Feeling guilty, ashamed, and inadequate due to chronic lateness.
7. Physical Health Issues: Increased risk of cardiovascular disease, diabetes, and other health problems.

Why We're Consistently Late

1. Poor Time Estimation: Underestimating time required for tasks and travel.

2. Procrastination: Delaying tasks until the last minute.

3. Distractions: Getting sidetracked by social media, email, or other non-essential activities.

4. Perfectionism: Spending too much time on details, leading to tardiness.

5. Lack of Prioritization: Failing to prioritize tasks and focus on essential activities.

6. Avoidance: Using lateness as a coping mechanism for anxiety or fear.

7. Habits: Engaging in habitual behaviors that contribute to tardiness.

Overcoming Consistent Lateness

1. Set Realistic Goals: Establish achievable deadlines and schedules.

2. Prioritize Tasks: Focus on essential activities and minimize distractions.

3. Use Time-Management Tools: Leverage calendars, planners, and apps to stay organized.

4. Leave Early: Plan to arrive early to account for unexpected delays.

5. Avoid Multitasking: Focus on one task at a time to maintain productivity.

6. Seek Accountability: Share schedules and goals with a friend or mentor for support.

7. Practice Mindfulness: Stay present and focused to avoid procrastination.

Consistent lateness can have severe consequences on our lives, relationships, and well-being. By understanding the reasons behind this behavior and implementing strategies for change, we can overcome chronic tardiness and develop healthier habits. Remember, punctuality is a skill that can be developed with practice and patience – start making a change today.

The Dangers of Overindulging: How Excessive Behavior Can Harm Your Health and Happiness

Overindulging, a common pitfall in today's world, can have severe consequences on our physical and mental well-being, relationships, and overall quality of life.

The Consequences of Overindulging

Overindulging can lead to:

1. Health Problems: Weight gain, increased risk of chronic diseases, and compromised immune function.
2. Mental Health Issues: Depression, anxiety, and decreased self-esteem.
3. Strained Relationships: Damaged connections with loved ones due to excessive behavior.
4. Financial Consequences: Debt, financial stress, and reduced savings.
5. Decreased Productivity: Reduced focus, motivation, and performance in work and personal life.
6. Guilt and Shame: Negative emotions and self-criticism following excessive behavior.
7. Loss of Control: Feeling powerless to stop or control excessive behavior.

Why We Overindulge

1. Emotional Coping Mechanism: Using excessive behavior to cope with stress, emotions, or trauma.

2. Social Pressure: Succumbing to peer pressure or societal expectations.

3. Lack of Self-Care: Neglecting physical, emotional, and mental needs.

4. Instant Gratification: Prioritizing short-term pleasure over long-term consequences.

5. Habits and Triggers: Engaging in automatic behaviors or responding to triggers without awareness.

Breaking the Cycle of Overindulging

1. Self-Awareness: Recognizing patterns and triggers of excessive behavior.

2. Set Boundaries: Establishing limits and guidelines for behavior.

3. Healthy Alternatives: Replacing excessive behavior with nourishing habits.

4. Seek Support: Surrounding yourself with positive influences and support systems.

5. Mindfulness and Self-Compassion: Practicing present-moment awareness and kindness towards yourself.

6. Gradual Change: Implementing small, sustainable changes towards healthier habits.

7. Forgiveness and Self-Care: Treating yourself with kindness and prioritizing self-care.

Overindulging can have severe consequences on our lives, but by understanding the reasons behind this behavior and implementing strategies for change, we can develop healthier habits and improve our overall well-being. Remember, breaking the cycle of overindulging takes time, patience, and self-compassion – start your journey towards a more balanced life today.

The Devastating Consequences of a Sedentary Lifestyle: Why Exercise is Essential for a Healthy Life

A lack of exercise, a common phenomenon in today's world, can have severe consequences on our physical and mental health, relationships, and overall quality of life.

The Consequences of a Sedentary Lifestyle

A lack of exercise can lead to:

1. Chronic Diseases: Increased risk of heart disease, diabetes, and some cancers.
2. Weight Gain and Obesity: Excess weight and body fat, leading to various health problems.
3. Mental Health Issues: Depression, anxiety, and decreased self-esteem.
4. Reduced Strength and Flexibility: Decreased muscle mass and flexibility, making daily tasks more challenging.
5. Poor Sleep Quality: Insomnia, daytime fatigue, and other sleep-related issues.
6. Decreased Bone Density: Increased risk of osteoporosis and fractures.
7. Reduced Immune Function: Weakened immune system, making us more susceptible to illnesses.

Why We Don't Exercise

1. Lack of Time: Busy schedules and prioritizing other activities over exercise.

2. Motivation and Interest: Struggling to find enjoyable physical activities or lacking motivation.

3. Health Concerns: Fear of injury or exacerbating existing health conditions.

4. Environmental Factors: Limited access to safe exercise spaces or facilities.

5. Sedentary Lifestyle Habits: Spending excessive time on screens or engaging in other inactive behaviors.

The Benefits of Exercise

1. Improved Physical Health: Reduced risk of chronic diseases, weight management, and increased strength and flexibility.

2. Enhanced Mental Health: Reduced stress, anxiety, and depression, improved mood and self-esteem.

3. Increased Energy Levels: Boosted energy and reduced fatigue.

4. Better Sleep Quality: Improved sleep duration, quality, and consistency.

5. Social Benefits: Opportunities to meet new people, build relationships, and develop a sense of community.

Incorporating Exercise into Your Life

1. Start Small: Begin with short, manageable sessions and gradually increase duration and intensity.

2. Find Enjoyable Activities: Engage in physical activities that bring you joy, such as walking, dancing, or swimming.

3. Schedule Exercise: Prioritize exercise by scheduling it into your daily routine.

4. Seek Support: Exercise with friends, family, or a personal trainer for motivation and accountability.

5. Monitor Progress: Track your progress, celebrate milestones, and adjust your routine as needed.

A lack of exercise can have severe consequences on our lives, but by understanding the reasons behind it and incorporating physical activity into our daily routine, we can improve our overall health, happiness, and well-being. Remember, every small step counts – start your journey towards a healthier life today.

The Devastating Consequences of Poor Sleep Habits: Why Quality Sleep is Essential for a Healthy Life

Poor sleep habits, a common phenomenon in today's fast-paced world, can have severe consequences on our physical and mental health, relationships, and overall quality of life.

The Consequences of Poor Sleep Habits

Poor sleep habits can lead to:

1. Impaired Cognitive Function: Reduced concentration, memory, and decision-making skills.

2. Mood Disorders: Increased risk of depression, anxiety, and mood swings.

3. Cardiovascular Disease: Higher risk of heart attacks, strokes, and high blood pressure.

4. Weakened Immune System: Reduced ability to fight off infections and diseases.

5. Weight Gain and Obesity: Disrupted appetite hormones, leading to weight gain and obesity.

6. Premature Aging: Accelerated aging process, including wrinkles, fine lines, and age spots.

7. Reduced Reaction Time and Motor Function: Slowed reaction times and impaired motor function.

Why We Develop Poor Sleep Habits

1. Irregular Sleep Schedule: Unpredictable sleep patterns, making it difficult for the body to establish a natural rhythm.
2. Stimulating Activities Before Bedtime: Engaging in stimulating activities, such as watching TV or scrolling through phones, before bedtime.
3. Caffeine and Nicotine Consumption: Consuming caffeine and nicotine in the afternoon or evening.
4. Electronic Device Use Before Bedtime: Exposure to screens and electronic devices before bedtime.
5. Stress and Anxiety: Allowing stress and anxiety to interfere with sleep.
6. Uncomfortable Sleep Environment: Sleeping in an environment that is too hot, cold, or uncomfortable.

Prioritizing Quality Sleep

1. Establish a Consistent Sleep Schedule: Set a regular sleep schedule and stick to it.
2. Create a Relaxing Bedtime Routine: Engage in calming activities, such as reading or meditation, before bedtime.
3. Optimize Your Sleep Environment: Create a dark, quiet, and cool sleep environment.
4. Avoid Stimulating Activities Before Bedtime: Avoid stimulating activities, such as exercise or watching TV, before bedtime.
5. Limit Electronic Device Use Before Bedtime: Avoid using electronic devices at least an hour before bedtime.
6. Manage Stress and Anxiety: Practice stress-reducing techniques, such as deep breathing or yoga, to manage stress and anxiety.

Poor sleep habits can have severe consequences on our lives, but by understanding the reasons behind them and prioritizing quality sleep, we can improve our overall health, happiness, and well-being. Remember, quality sleep is essential for a healthy life – make it a priority tonight.

The Hidden Dangers of Cluttering: How Clutter Affects Our Minds, Bodies, and Lives

Cluttering, a common phenomenon in today's consumerist society, can have severe consequences on our mental and physical health, relationships, and overall quality of life.

The Consequences of Cluttering

Cluttering can lead to:

1. Increased Stress and Anxiety: Cluttered environments can contribute to feelings of overwhelm and anxiety.
2. Decreased Productivity: Clutter can make it difficult to focus and complete tasks efficiently.
3. Physical Health Problems: Clutter can lead to poor air quality, pest infestations, and tripping hazards.
4. Mental Health Issues: Clutter has been linked to depression, ADHD, and other mental health conditions.
5. Strained Relationships: Clutter can cause tension and conflict in relationships.
6. Financial Consequences: Clutter can lead to wasted resources, missed opportunities, and financial losses.
7. Lost Time and Energy: Clutter can consume time and energy, taking away from more important activities.

Why We Clutter

1. Emotional Attachment: We often attach emotional value to possessions, making it difficult to let go.
2. Fear of Loss: We fear that getting rid of items will lead to loss or regret.
3. Lack of Organization: Poor organizational skills can lead to clutter accumulation.
4. Consumerism: We are often encouraged to buy and accumulate more.
5. Trauma and Sentimentality: Clutter can be a coping mechanism for trauma or a way to hold onto memories.

The Benefits of Decluttering and Minimalism

1. Reduced Stress and Anxiety: Decluttering can lead to a sense of calm and relaxation.
2. Increased Productivity: Minimalism can improve focus and efficiency.
3. Improved Physical Health: Decluttering can lead to better air quality, reduced allergens, and improved safety.
4. Mental Clarity and Focus: Minimalism can improve mental clarity and focus.
5. Stronger Relationships: Decluttering can lead to more harmonious relationships.
6. Financial Savings: Minimalism can lead to reduced waste, savings, and increased financial security.
7. More Time and Energy: Decluttering can free up time and energy for more important activities.

Decluttering and Minimalism Strategies

1. Start Small: Begin with small areas or categories of items.
2. Sort and Purge: Sort items into categories and purge unnecessary items.
3. Organize and Categorize: Organize remaining items into categories and assign a home.

4. Create Habits: Create habits and routines to maintain minimalism.
5. Seek Support: Seek support from friends, family, or professionals.

Cluttering can have severe consequences on our lives, but by understanding the reasons behind it and adopting decluttering and minimalism strategies, we can improve our mental and physical health, relationships, and overall quality of life. Remember, minimalism is a journey – start decluttering today and discover a more organized, peaceful, and fulfilling life.

The Consequences of Avoiding Responsibility: How Shunning Accountability Can Harm Our Lives and Relationships

Avoiding responsibility, a common behavior in today's society, can have severe consequences on our personal growth, relationships, and overall well-being.

The Consequences of Avoiding Responsibility

Avoiding responsibility can lead to:

1. Stunted Personal Growth: Failure to take ownership of actions and decisions hinders self-awareness and development.
2. Damaged Relationships: Shunning accountability can lead to mistrust, resentment, and conflict in personal and professional relationships.
3. Missed Opportunities: Avoiding responsibility can result in missed chances for learning, growth, and success.
4. Increased Stress and Anxiety: Dodging accountability can lead to feelings of guilt, shame, and anxiety.
5. Lack of Trust and Credibility: Consistently avoiding responsibility can erode trust and credibility with others.
6. Decreased Self-Esteem: Shunning accountability can lead to negative self-perception and low self-esteem.
7. Inability to Set Boundaries: Avoiding responsibility can make it challenging to establish and maintain healthy boundaries.

Why We Avoid Responsibility

1. *Fear of Failure: Fear of making mistakes or facing consequences.*
2. *Lack of Self-Awareness: Limited understanding of one's actions and their impact.*
3. *Avoidance of Emotional Pain: Dodging accountability to avoid feelings of guilt, shame, or anxiety.*
4. *Perfectionism: Unrealistic expectations and fear of not meeting them.*
5. *Upbringing and Environment: Learned behavior from family or surroundings.*
6. *Trauma and Past Experiences: Using avoidance as a coping mechanism for past traumas.*

Embracing Responsibility

1. *Self-Reflection and Awareness: Understanding actions, decisions, and their consequences.*
2. *Accountability Partners: Surrounding yourself with people who encourage accountability.*
3. *Setting Boundaries: Establishing clear limits and expectations.*
4. *Embracing Failure: Viewing failures as opportunities for growth and learning.*
5. *Practicing Mindfulness: Being present and aware in daily life.*
6. *Developing Emotional Intelligence: Understanding and managing emotions.*
7. *Seeking Feedback: Encouraging constructive criticism and feedback.*

Avoiding responsibility can have severe consequences on our lives and relationships. By understanding the reasons behind this behavior and embracing accountability, we can foster personal growth, build trust, and develop healthier relationships. Remember, taking ownership of our actions and decisions is the first step towards a more authentic, responsible, and fulfilling life.

The Dangers of Overcommitting: How Taking on Too Much Can Harm Our Lives and Relationships

Overcommitting, a common pitfall in today's fast-paced world, can have severe consequences on our mental and physical health, relationships, and overall well-being.

The Consequences of Overcommitting

Overcommitting can lead to:

1. Burnout and Exhaustion: Physical, emotional, and mental depletion.
2. Strained Relationships: Damaged connections with family, friends, and colleagues due to unmet expectations.
3. Decreased Productivity: Reduced focus, efficiency, and quality of work.
4. Increased Stress and Anxiety: Feelings of overwhelm, guilt, and inadequacy.
5. Poor Time Management: Inability to prioritize tasks, leading to missed deadlines and opportunities.
6. Lack of Self-Care: Neglect of personal needs, hobbies, and interests.
7. Decreased Creativity and Innovation: Stifled imagination and problem-solving skills.

Why We Overcommit

1. Fear of Missing Out (FOMO): Fear of missing opportunities or experiences.

2. People-Pleasing: Desire to satisfy others' expectations and needs.

3. Perfectionism: Unrealistic standards and fear of not meeting them.

4. Lack of Boundaries: Failure to set clear limits and priorities.

5. Overestimation of Capabilities: Misjudging one's time, energy, and resources.

6. Trauma and Past Experiences: Using overcommitting as a coping mechanism for past traumas.

Setting Healthy Boundaries

1. Self-Awareness and Reflection: Understanding personal limits, values, and priorities.

2. Prioritization and Focus: Concentrating on essential tasks and activities.

3. Communication and Assertiveness: Clearly expressing needs, boundaries, and expectations.

4. Learning to Say No: Politely declining non-essential commitments.

5. Seeking Support and Delegation: Sharing responsibilities and seeking help when needed.

6. Embracing Imperfection and Flexibility: Accepting limitations and adapting to changing circumstances.

7. Practicing Self-Compassion and Mindfulness: Treating oneself with kindness and staying present.

Overcommitting can have severe consequences on our lives and relationships. By understanding the reasons behind this behavior and setting healthy boundaries, we can maintain a balance between commitments and personal well-being. Remember, prioritizing oneself is not selfish – it's essential.

The Power of Gratitude: How a Lack of Appreciation Can Negatively Impact Our Lives

Gratitude is a vital component of a happy and fulfilling life. However, many of us often overlook the importance of gratitude, leading to a lack of appreciation for the good things in our lives.

The Consequences of a Lack of Gratitude

A lack of gratitude can lead to:

1. Negative Relationships: Strained connections with family, friends, and colleagues due to unappreciative behavior.
2. Increased Stress and Anxiety: Focus on what's lacking rather than what's present, leading to feelings of overwhelm.
3. Decreased Self-Esteem: Failure to recognize and appreciate personal achievements and strengths.
4. Poor Physical Health: Weakened immune system, increased blood pressure, and other health issues.
5. Mental Health Concerns: Depression, anxiety disorders, and other mental health issues.
6. Lack of Empathy and Compassion: Reduced ability to understand and connect with others.
7. Missed Opportunities: Failure to recognize and capitalize on opportunities due to a lack of appreciation.

Why We Lack Gratitude

1. Entitlement Mentality: Expecting good things without appreciation or effort.
2. Comparison and Envy: Focusing on what others have rather than what we have.
3. Negative Thinking Patterns: Dwelling on what's lacking rather than what's present.
4. Trauma and Past Experiences: Using a lack of gratitude as a coping mechanism for past traumas.
5. Social Media and Consumerism: Constant exposure to advertisements and curated highlight reels.

Cultivating Gratitude

1. Gratitude Journaling: Writing down things you're thankful for each day.
2. Mindfulness and Presence: Focusing on the present moment and appreciating its beauty.
3. Sharing Gratitude with Others: Expressing appreciation to those who deserve it.
4. Reframing Negative Thoughts: Focusing on the positive aspects of challenging situations.
5. Practicing Self-Care and Self-Compassion: Treating yourself with kindness and appreciation.
6. Seeking Out Positive Influences: Surrounding yourself with supportive and grateful individuals.
7. Embracing Imperfection and Uncertainty: Finding gratitude in life's uncertainties and imperfections.

A lack of gratitude can have severe consequences on our lives and relationships. By understanding the reasons behind this behavior and cultivating a grateful mindset, we can improve our mental and physical health, relationships, and overall well-being. Remember, gratitude is a muscle that must be exercised regularly to see results. Start practicing gratitude today and discover a more fulfilling life.

The Dangers of Comparison: How Measuring Yourself Against Others Can Harm Your Mental Health and Happiness

Comparing oneself to others is a natural human tendency, but it can have severe consequences on our mental health, happiness, and overall well-being.

The Consequences of Comparison

Comparing oneself to others can lead to:

1. Decreased Self-Esteem: Constantly feeling inadequate and inferior to others.
2. Anxiety and Depression: Increased stress and feelings of hopelessness.
3. Unrealistic Expectations: Setting unattainable goals and feeling disappointed.
4. Missed Opportunities: Focusing on what others have rather than pursuing personal goals.
5. Strained Relationships: Jealousy, resentment, and damaged connections.
6. Lack of Authenticity: Trying to emulate others rather than being true to oneself.
7. Stunted Personal Growth: Focusing on external validation rather than self-improvement.

Why We Compare Ourselves to Others

1. Social Media and Consumerism: Constant exposure to curated highlight reels and advertisements.

2. Fear of Missing Out (FOMO): Fear of missing opportunities or experiences.

3. Insecurities and Self-Doubt: Using comparison as a coping mechanism for personal insecurities.

4. Competition and Envy: Feeling the need to compete with others and coveting what they have.

5. Lack of Self-Awareness and Purpose: Unclear personal values and goals.

The Benefits of Focusing on Personal Growth

1. Increased Self-Esteem and Confidence: Focusing on personal strengths and achievements.

2. Improved Mental Health and Happiness: Reduced stress and increased feelings of fulfillment.

3. Authenticity and Individuality: Embracing unique qualities and strengths.

4. Meaningful Relationships: Building connections based on shared values and interests.

5. Personal Growth and Development: Pursuing goals and passions.

6. Increased Resilience and Adaptability: Focusing on progress rather than perfection.

7. Greater Purpose and Direction: Clear personal values and goals.

Breaking the Comparison Habit

1. Self-Reflection and Awareness: Recognizing personal comparison habits.

2. Mindfulness and Presence: Focusing on the present moment.

3. Gratitude and Appreciation: Practicing gratitude for personal strengths and blessings.

4. Personal Goal-Setting and Progress Tracking: Focusing on personal growth.

5. Seeking Support and Community: Surrounding yourself with positive influences.

6. Embracing Imperfection and Uncertainty: Accepting and learning from mistakes.

7. Practicing Self-Compassion and Kindness: Treating yourself with kindness and understanding.

Comparing oneself to others can have severe consequences on our mental health, happiness, and overall well-being. By understanding the reasons behind this behavior and focusing on personal growth and self-improvement, we can break the comparison habit and cultivate a more authentic, fulfilling life. Remember, personal growth is a journey, not a competition.

The Paralyzing Grip of Fear: How Fear of Change Holds Us Back from Growth and Happiness

Fear of change is a ubiquitous and insidious force that can hold us back from realizing our full potential and living a fulfilling life.

The Reasons Behind Fear of Change

1. Uncertainty and Unknown Outcomes: Fear of the unknown and unpredictable consequences of change.
2. Loss of Control and Security: Fear of losing control and security in the face of change.
3. Past Experiences and Trauma: Past experiences and trauma that have led to a fear of change.
4. Comfort Zone and Familiarity: Fear of leaving the comfort zone and familiarity of current circumstances.
5. Social and Cultural Pressures: Fear of change due to social and cultural pressures and expectations.

The Consequences of Fear of Change

1. Stagnation and Complacency: Lack of growth and progress due to fear of change.
2. Missed Opportunities and Regret: Missing out on opportunities and experiencing regret due to fear of change.
3. Anxiety and Stress: Increased anxiety and stress due to fear of change.

4. Limited Potential and Happiness: Limiting one's potential and happiness due to fear of change.
5. Strained Relationships and Communication: Strained relationships and communication due to fear of change.

Overcoming Fear of Change

1. Self-Awareness and Reflection: Recognizing and understanding one's fear of change.
2. Reframing Perspective and Mindset: Reframing one's perspective and mindset to view change as an opportunity.
3. Building Resilience and Adaptability: Building resilience and adaptability to navigate change.
4. Seeking Support and Guidance: Seeking support and guidance from others to navigate change.
5. Taking Small Steps and Embracing Progress: Taking small steps towards change and embracing progress.
6. Practicing Mindfulness and Presence: Practicing mindfulness and presence to stay grounded in the face of change.
7. Embracing Uncertainty and Imperfection: Embracing uncertainty and imperfection as a natural part of change.

Fear of change is a natural and normal part of life, but it can hold us back from realizing our full potential and living a fulfilling life. By understanding the reasons behind fear of change and implementing strategies to overcome it, we can build resilience, adaptability, and a growth mindset. Remember, change is an opportunity for growth, learning, and happiness – embrace it.